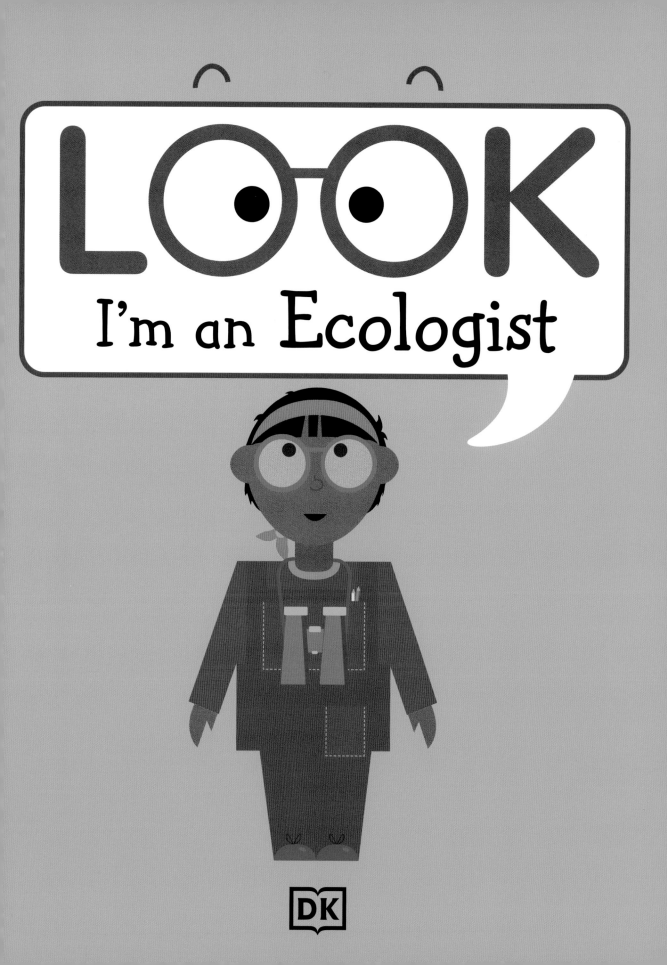

LOOK
I'm an Ecologist

DK

For the grown-ups

This book is full of hands-on activities that will tap straight into your child's natural curiosity. Each activity is designed to let your child play and learn with all their senses. Together, you can grow their love of nature and science, as well as their understanding of the world.

Here are a few tips to help you along the way:

Your child should be supervised at all times when carrying out activities and experiments, but try to give them time and space to lead the direction of play. The questions in this book are suggestions. Let your child ask, and answer, their own questions.

•

Involve your child in each step of the projects. Let them measure, mix, and follow the instructions. Encourage your child to work things out, and allow them to modify the activity if they would like to.

•

Adult Alert stars show where your child will need extra grown-up help. Before you start an activity, consider any hazards together and ways to avoid them. If your child has long hair, make sure it is tied back and out of the way.

Adult ALERT!

•

Protect the area where your child will be playing and encourage them to wear old clothes or an apron. Being prepared lets your child enjoy themselves to their fullest. Making a mess is part of the fun and learning!

DK Penguin Random House

Written by Cathriona Hickey
Editors Sarah MacLeod, Sophie Parkes
Senior Editor Dawn Sirett
Design and Illustration Rachael Hare
Additional Design Karen Hood
Educational Consultant Penny Coltman
Photographer Lol Johnson
Jacket Designer Rachael Hare
Jacket Coordinator Issy Walsh
Production Editor Abi Maxwell
Production Controller Isabell Schart
Managing Editor Penny Smith
Deputy Art Director Mabel Chan
Publishing Director Sarah Larter

First published in Great Britain in 2021 by
Dorling Kindersley Limited
One Embassy Gardens, 8 Viaduct Gardens,
London, SW11 7BW

The authorised representative in the EEA is
Dorling Kindersley Verlag GmbH. Arnulfstr. 124,
80636 Munich, Germany

Copyright © 2021 Dorling Kindersley Limited
A Penguin Random House Company
10 9 8 7 6 5 4 3 2 1
001-322923-Sep/2021

A CIP catalogue record for this book
is available from the British Library.
ISBN: 978-0-2414-8432-6

Printed and bound in China

www.dk.com

Picture credits
The publisher would like to thank the following for their kind permission to reproduce their photographs:
(Key: a-above; b-below/bottom; c-centre; f-far; l-left; r-right; t-top)

6 123RF.com: stillfx (cra). 10 Dorling Kindersley: Neil Fletcher (br). Dreamstime.com: Vvoevale (c). 11 Dreamstime.com: Ksushsh (tc, cra); Vvoevale (ca). 12 Dreamstime.com: Anton Starikov (ca). 14 123RF.com: Ruslan Nassyrov (cla). 15 123RF.com: Ruslan Nassyrov (b). 16 123RF.com: Ruslan Nassyrov (cra). 17 Dreamstime.com: Stig Karlsson / Stigsfoto (cb). 20-21 Dreamstime.com: Daboost. 21 Alamy Stock Photo: Andrew Paterson (clb). Dreamstime.com: Toneimage (c). 22 Dreamstime.com: Veronika Oliinyk (cla, cra). 22-23 Dreamstime.com: Isselee (bc). 23 Alamy Stock Photo: blickwinkel / H. Schulz (bc); Sean Campbell (bl); blickwinkel / Schulz (fbr). Dreamstime.com: Isselee (br); Veronika Oliinyk (tr, crb). Getty Images / iStock: Kaphoto (bc/Badger). 28 123RF.com: Václav Šebek (br). Dreamstime.com: Victortyakht (bc). 29 123RF.com: Christian Mueringer (cr). Alamy Stock Photo: Tom Uhlman (bl). 31 Alamy Stock Photo: Philip Jones (bc). 32 Dreamstime.com: Elena Kazanskaya (cra). 34 Dreamstime.com: Katerynabibro (cra). 36 Dreamstime.com: Marina Lohrbach (br). 37 Dreamstime.com: Richard J Thompson / Photoaged (cla); Krzysztof Slusarczyk (br). 38 Dreamstime.com: Katerynabibro (c/bean); Phanuwatn (cla); Anton Starikov (c). 40 Dreamstime.com: Carolyn Franks (cla); Liudmyla Havryliuk (c); Penchan Pumila (cr). 41 Dreamstime.com: Carolyn Franks (ca); David Moreno (tc); Tatiana Neelova (bl); Wirestock (bc). 45 123RF.com: (cl); Martin Spurny (c). Dreamstime.com: Photka (c/Trash, bc); Svitlana Ponurkina (tl); Roberto Giovannini / HP_Proprietario (crb)

Cover images: Front: Dreamstime.com: Michael Truchon clb

All other images © Dorling Kindersley
For further information see: www.dkimages.com

MIX
Paper from
responsible sources
FSC™ C018179

Contents

Little minds have big ideas!

Ecologists study **plants**, **animals**, and the places where they live, called **environments**. You can be an ecologist too! You just need to ask **questions,** and use **your brain** and **your senses** to answer them

Curious questions

Start thinking like an ecologist! Here are some questions to ask yourself as you play.

- When I see or hear an animal, what is it doing? Is it calling to other animals? Is it looking for food? Is it building a nest? Is it hiding to keep itself safe?

- When I look at a plant, what can I see? Are new shoots growing? Have animals been eating it? Does it look like it needs water? Do the flowers on it smell nice? How might that help the plant?

- Are there things I can do to help plants and animals?

Your ecologist senses

Brain
Your brain is not one of your senses, but it gathers information from them all and helps you understand it.

Hearing
Animals make lots of noises. Listen carefully when you are outside. What can you hear?

Sight
Awesome ecologists use their eyes to spot animal clues, such as paw prints, spider's webs, or frogspawn.

Smell
Nature is full of interesting smells. Use your nose to smell flowers, soil, or wet leaves.

Taste
Your tongue is great at tasting different food flavours. Try growing some herbs to add to your food.

Touch
Your skin tells you how things feel. Be careful with plants that might be prickly and animals that might sting.

Let's go explore the world around us!

Nature treasures

A **nature walk** is a great way to **see** nature. Collect **treasures** such as leaves, fallen flowers, and feathers. Use them in these crafts to **remember** what you found.

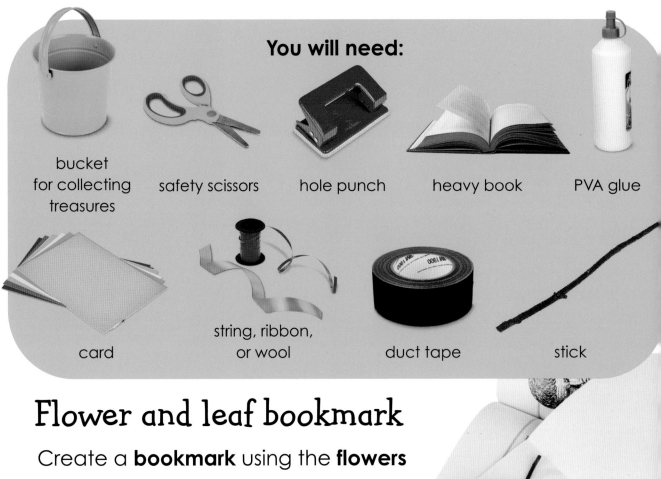

You will need:

bucket for collecting treasures

safety scissors

hole punch

heavy book

PVA glue

card

string, ribbon, or wool

duct tape

stick

Flower and leaf bookmark

Create a **bookmark** using the **flowers** and **leaves** you find on your walk.

1 Carefully lay the **flowers** and **leaves** between two pieces of **card**. Then put the card in between the pages of a **heavy book** and close it.

2

After a few days, take the **flowers** and **leaves** out of the book. Be very careful – they will be **fragile**!

Adult ALERT!

3

Use **safety scissors** to **cut** a piece of **card** about 5 cm (2 in) wide by 20 cm (8 in) long.

Use a hole punch to make a hole in the top of the card and tie a piece of string, ribbon, or wool through the hole.

4

Make a **beautiful design** on the card with the pressed flowers and leaves, then **glue** them in place.

7

Nature memory stick

A **memory stick** is perfect for keeping a **collection** of things you find on your nature walk.

1

Put dots of **glue** along the stick where you want to place your nature treasures. Then gently **press** the treasures onto the glue.

2

Tie **string, ribbon, or wool** to the stick for extra decoration. You can plant your stick in a **flower pot** and display it in your room.

Collect treasures that have different colours and textures.

Beautiful bracelet

This **sticky bracelet** is a great way to **collect** nature treasures as you go!

1

Ask an adult to wrap a length of **duct tape** around your wrist with the **sticky side out** and join the ends to make a loop.

Adult ALERT!

2

Go on a nature walk to **collect** fallen leaves, flowers, feathers, and twigs. **Press** each treasure you find onto your sticky bracelet.

By the end of your adventure, you will have a bracelet full of the beautiful things you found along the way.

9

Wonderful trees!

There are so many **types of trees** in the world.
Let's use **art** to see how they are **different**!

You will need:

paint

paintbrushes

PVA glue

crayons

paper

fallen leaves

Take paper and coloured crayons with you on a walk.

Smooth beech bark

Bumpy willow bark

Bark clues

Lean your paper against the **bark** of a tree. **Rub** the side of your **crayon** on the paper. What happens? Try another tree – does it look different?

1 Leaf clues

Collect fallen leaves that are different **colours, shapes, and sizes.** At home, leave the leaves to dry if they are wet.

The leaves of each type of tree look different.

2

Paint the leaves in your favourite colours, then leave them to dry. **Arrange** your leaves on a piece of **paper** and stick them down with glue.

What shapes are your leaves?

Long and wide with wavy edges

Long and thin with smooth edges

Start a nature gallery to display your tree art!

Who is it?

How many different **minibeasts** can you **name**?
Collect minibeasts from the **garden** or **park**
and see if you can name them all.

You will need:

shallow plastic container

soil

magnifying glass

paper

leaves and moss

small pebbles

1

Put a thin layer of **soil** in the plastic container. Add **pebbles**, **leaves**, and **moss**.

2

In the park or garden, **look** for a minibeast under dead wood, stones, or leaves. **Lay** the paper next to the animal and **wait** for it to crawl onto the paper.

ADULT ALERT!

You MUST put the animal back safely where you found it as soon as you've looked at it.

3

Once it is on the paper, **carefully** place the minibeast in your container.

EXPLORE ecology

How many legs does the minibeast have?

Let it crawl on your hand. How does it feel?

How many body parts can you name?

Look closely at the animal with a magnifying glass.

A snack for the birds

During winter it can be tricky for **birds** to find **food**. **Help** the birds when they need it most by making these two tasty **birdfeeders**.

For the pine cone feeder, you will need:

pine cone

peanut butter

seeds

string and safety scissors

shallow container

wooden knife

1

Pine cone feeder

Wrap a length of **string** around the wider end of the pine cone and **tie a knot**.

Use about 60 cm (24 in) of string.

2

Use the wooden knife to **smother** the pine cone with a thick layer of **peanut butter**.

Hang your finished feeder from a branch outside, then stand back and watch the birds that come to use it.

How many different types of birds use your feeder? Are they big or small? What colours are they?

3

Pour your seeds into the container and **roll** your pine cone in the seeds. **Hang** the feeder outside.

Make sure your feeder is tied on well!

If you don't have peanut butter

or a pine cone, keep the birds
well fed with this bottle feeder.

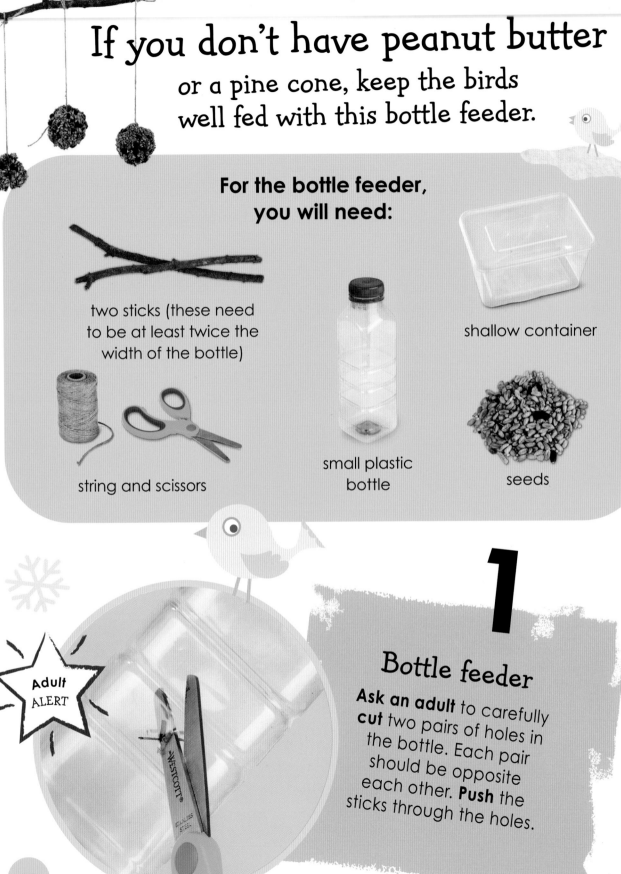

For the bottle feeder,
you will need:

two sticks (these need
to be at least twice the
width of the bottle)

shallow container

string and scissors

small plastic
bottle

seeds

Adult
ALERT

1

Bottle feeder

Ask an adult to carefully
cut two pairs of holes in
the bottle. Each pair
should be opposite
each other. **Push** the
sticks through the holes.

2 Above each stick, cut a feeding hole about 1 cm (0.4 in) wide. **Fill** the bottle with **seeds** and screw the lid on.

Try using a mix of different seeds.

Try using different types of seeds or nuts in your feeder. Do some birds prefer one thing over another?

Woodpeckers love peanuts

Tie a long piece of string around the bottle and hang it outside for birds to perch on.

17

Minibeast home

Minibeasts like a **home** that provides them with **food**, **shelter**, and **water**. This **minibeast habitat** provides a place for different animals to live together.

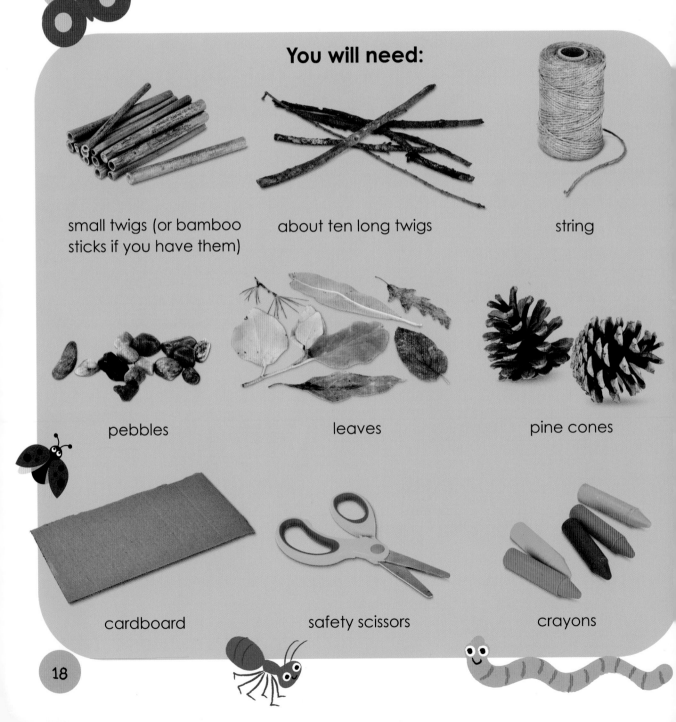

You will need:

small twigs (or bamboo sticks if you have them)

about ten long twigs

string

pebbles

leaves

pine cones

cardboard

safety scissors

crayons

1

Find a patch of soil outside. Arrange the **long twigs** in a cone shape. **Tie string** around the top to hold the sticks together.

2

Lay the **pebbles** inside your habitat, then layer small **twigs** or **bamboo sticks**, **pine cones**, and **leaves** on top.

Shhh! After a few days, peek inside to see who has moved in!

Cut out a triangle of cardboard for a door.

19

What's the weather like?

Recording the **weather** and learning how **animals** and **plants** cope in different conditions is an important part of being an ecologist.

You will need a notebook with seven pages, or a large piece of paper.

Label each page with each day of the week and the date, like this:

Adult ALERT

Ask an adult for help if you find writing tricky.

Monday

DATE _____

Do you see sun? Do you feel rain or snow? Do you hear wind?

Look outside. What is the weather like? What do you **see**, **feel**, and **hear**?

Watch the weather for seven days. Does it **change**?

Draw or **write** about the weather in your notebook.

How do you get **ready** for the weather? Do you wear **boots** if it rains? Do you wear a **hat** if it's sunny?

How do animals protect themselves in different types of weather?

Can you see any animals enjoying the weather?

Draw a picture of an **animal** that likes the rain and one that likes the sun.

Mud prints

Animals and ecologists **love** mud!
Animals like to **roll in it** and ecologists like to **look in it** to **learn all about them.**

You will need:

plastic animals

mixing bowl

cocoa powder

water

flour

Mix everything together to make a **thick** mud.

Place the **ingredients** in your **bowl.**

Leave the mixture to dry a little.

Walk your plastic animals through the **mud**. Think about what they would do in the wild – birds **hop**, horses **trot**, and goats **charge**!

Next time you are on a nature walk, look out for tracks in the mud. Can you spot the tracks of a deer, badger, or fox? What do your tracks look like?

Hide your animals and ask someone to **guess** which animal made each **track**. Give them clues – heavier animals leave deeper prints.

Deer prints

Badger prints

Fox prints

Spider weave

Spiders build **webs** to **catch** bugs to eat. Can you **weave** a string web to **trap** a tasty treat?

You will need:

string

safety scissors

sticks

1 Lay your sticks so they **cross over** each other and make a **star shape**.

The bigger the sticks, the bigger the web!

2 **Wrap** and **tie** lengths of **string** around the sticks where they meet in the **middle**. Do this across each of the **diagonals**.

3 **Tie** a **very long** piece of **string** to a stick near the centre of the star. Then **wrap** the string around the next stick.

Hang your web from a tree in the garden or doorway in your house.

4 Continue, **twisting** the string around each stick until you reach the **edge** of the star. When you reach the end, tie a **knot**.

Did you know spiders are arachnids, not insects? Arachnids have eight legs, while insects have just six.

Nest building

Chicks need a **safe** and **sturdy** place to **hatch** and be **fed** by their parents. Let's see if you can build a **strong nest** of your own!

You will need:

paper plate

safety scissors

hole punch

air dry clay

nest materials

small sticks

1

Make **holes** around the **edge** of the plate. The holes should be about a **finger width** apart.

EXPLORE ecology

Does your nest feel safe and strong?

How deep does it need to be to keep the eggs safe?

What happens to the nest when it rains? Test it outside!

2

Weave sticks through the holes to create a **sturdy frame**.

Add leaves, moss, and feathers to make it soft and cosy.

Craft pretend eggs from air dry clay, and sit them in your nest like real eggs! Birds lay eggs in a nest and look after the chicks there when they hatch.

Sounds of nature

Can you make your **very own orchestra** from nature?
Head out on a **nature walk** to collect natural
bits and pieces to **use as instruments**.

Collect what you find in a bucket.

Animal sounds

Nature makes a lot of **noise**!
Wild animals will **make
a racket** for all sorts
of reasons.

Birds **sing** to **warn** other birds of danger.

Badgers **growl** when they **play**.

With your instruments:

Knock two together – do they make a sound?

Shake some of the things you find in a tin – what sounds do they make?

Can you make up a song about your walk and play along with your instruments?

Lots of things in nature can be instruments!

acorns

shake together

knock against a tree

chestnuts

pine cones

rub together

twigs

tap

leaves

stones

rustle

roll along the ground

seeds

rattle

29

Frog life cycle stone story

Paint your own froggy **life cycle** to see what it takes for **frogspawn** to grow into adult **frogs**.

You will need:

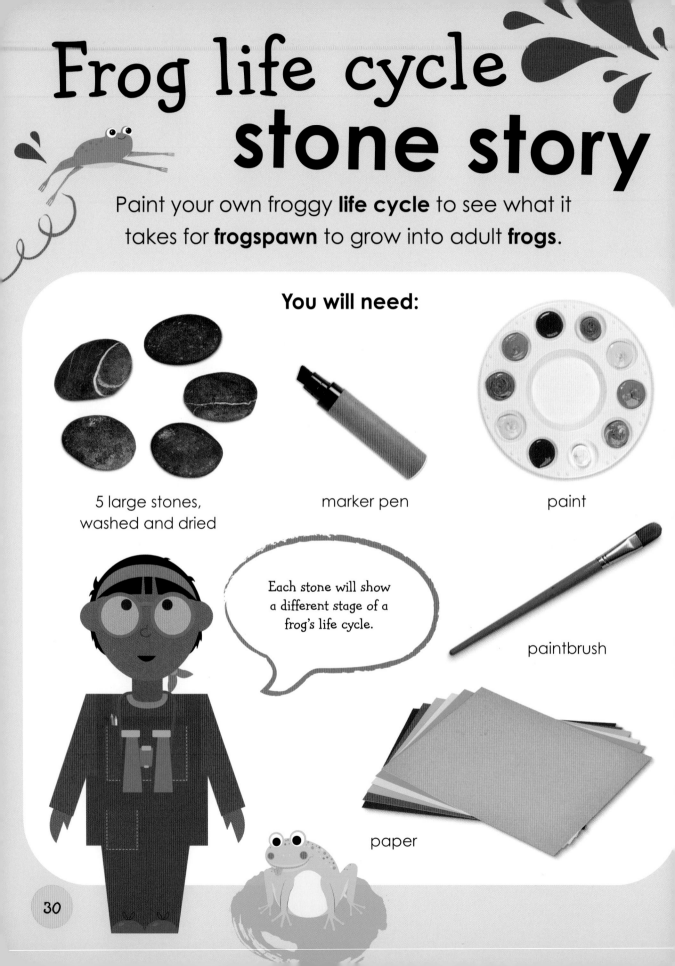

5 large stones, washed and dried

marker pen

paint

Each stone will show a different stage of a frog's life cycle.

paintbrush

paper

Paint

the five different stages
of a frog's life that
you see here.

What other life cycles can you paint?

frogspawn

tadpole

adult frog

Lay your stones in a
circle on a piece of
paper. Draw **arrows**
between each
stone to show which
way the **cycle** goes.

froglet

tadpole with legs

Next time you pass a
pond, look closely to see
if you can spot any of
the frog stages!

Frogs are **amphibians**. They can
live both in **water** and on **land**.
Changing from one form to
another, like from a tadpole to a
froglet, is called **metamorphosis**.
The frog looks completely
different at each stage!

31

Make your own soil!

Soil provides **energy** for **plants** to grow big and strong. You can make your own soil, called **compost**, using **leftover food**.

You will need:

paint

plastic container
with lid

pen

used coffee grounds

dead leaves

egg shells

fruit and vegetable
scraps

shredded
newspaper

cardboard

ADULT ALERT!

Use the **pen** to make **holes** in the **lid**. These will let **air** get to the compost.

Decorate your container

What's that smell? All the food and leaves in your compost are slowly breaking down. It can get pretty smelly!

Does the compost feel warm? This is because tiny organisms are working hard to break it down. In cold weather you might even see steam coming from it! Wash your hands after touching the compost.

Fill your box with the scraps, leaves, newspaper, egg shells, and cardboard, then put it **outside**. In a few months it will have **broken down** to form **nutrient-rich compost**!

Compost provides food to lots of living things, such as worms, bacteria (tiny organisms), and fungi.

Will it grow?

What do **plants** need to **grow**?
Let's grow some **beans** to find out.

What you will need:

3 tall glasses
(clear glass is best
so you can see the
bean sprout)

cotton wool

water

3 beans
(any bean seeds
will work, such as
broad beans)

1
Label your glasses
A, B, and C, and fill
each one two-thirds
full with **cotton wool**.
Place a **bean** in each
glass on top of the
cotton wool.

A

2
Sprinkle glasses
A and B with
water to **wet** the
cotton wool. Leave
the cotton wool
in glass C **dry**.

3

Leave each **glass** in the following places for **two weeks**:

Window sill

A

Window sill

Dark box or cupboard

B

C

4

Check on your beans **every few days**. Add more water to A and B if they look dry. Which bean grows **tallest**?

If you don't have any cotton wool, kitchen paper will work too!

A This bean has **water, light**, and **air** so it should grow the best.

B This bean should sprout, but it won't grow because it has **no light**.

C This bean should not sprout or grow because it has **no water**.

Flowers for bees and butterflies

Bees and **butterflies** love to feed on a delicious liquid called **nectar** that's found inside **flowers**. By growing flowers, you can help these **important insects**.

EXPLORE
ecology

Look outside for bees and butterflies. Which flowers do they go to? What colours are the flowers?

Do the flowers visited by bees and butterflies have a strong scent?

Can you draw and name the different parts of a flower?

pollen

stamen

petal

sepal

stem

echinacea

Here are some ideas for flowers you can grow that bees and butterflies love.

When you help bees and butterflies, you help plants, too! Without them, many plants wouldn't grow.

Feeding time

Butterflies and bees use their **long tongues** to drink **nectar** from flowers. As they feed, they rub against a **powder** on the flowers' stamens, called **pollen**, which **sticks** to their bodies.

Pollination

As the insects fly from **flower to flower**, the **pollen** on them is rubbed off onto parts of other flowers. This is called **pollination**. It helps plants to make **seeds** so new plants can grow.

sunflower

hemp agrimony

lavender

calendula

Paper plant pots

Growing plants is great fun, but to get started you need **pots**. Let's find out how to **make your own**.

You will need:

kitchen rolls cut in half

plastic container

newspaper or magazine

safety scissors

soil

seeds

drinking glass

Cardboard pots

Fold over each flap to cover the opening.

Cut four 2.5 cm (1 in) slits in one end of an empty half **kitchen roll** to create four **flaps. Repeat** with the other rolls.

Stand your **cardboard pots** in a **plastic container**. Fill them with **soil**, then they're ready for you to start **planting seeds**!

Newspaper pots

Take a sheet of **newspaper** and **fold** it twice lengthways.

Wrap the folded newspaper around a glass or bottle.

Fold the newspaper over the **base** of the glass, then remove the glass to leave your **newspaper pot**.

Try growing food in your pots. That means the food travels less to get to you, which is better for the planet.

Homegrown

Homegrown food is not only **good for the planet,** but **tastes delicious**, too – **let's get growing!**

You will need:

3 plant pots

compost

water

tomato seeds

red pepper seeds

basil seeds

1

Fill each pot three-quarters full with **compost**.

Compost is **packed** full of *nutrients*.

2

Push your **finger** into the compost to make a small **hole**.

3

Put the tomato **seeds** into a hole, then **cover** with a little compost. Do the same with the pepper and basil seeds in the other two pots.

4

Water the seeds, then place your pots on a **sunny** window sill.

Make sure you keep your compost moist. Check it each morning and add some water if it feels dry.

Try the food you have grown. What's your favourite?

When is your food is ready to pick?

Tomatoes and peppers should be plump and red and come off the stalk easily.

Basil leaves should be long and green.

Rocking rockpool

Rockpools are found on **rocky shores**. They form when **water gets trapped** on and between rocks as the **tide goes out**.

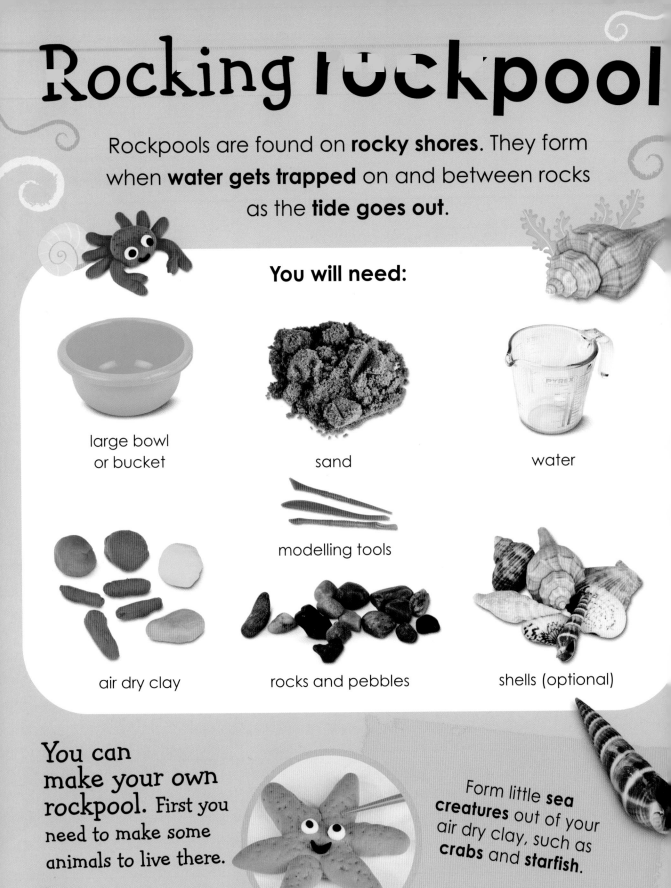

You will need:

large bowl or bucket

sand

water

modelling tools

air dry clay

rocks and pebbles

shells (optional)

You can make your own rockpool. First you need to make some animals to live there.

Form little **sea creatures** out of your air dry clay, such as **crabs** and **starfish**.

Let's build your rockpool

1

Spread a layer of **sand** in the **bowl**.

2

Place **rocks**, **pebbles** and **shells** around the edge of the sand. Pour in some **water**.

3

Now your animals are ready to **dive into** their **habitat**!

...you can add some **seaweed**!

If you live near the **seaside**...

Sea creatures live in rockpools, making a home until the sea comes back. An animal's home is called a habitat.

43

I can save the planet!

Our planet needs our **help!** Here are some ways we can all **protect the planet.**

Plastic in the oceans can harm sea creatures.

Try to buy food wrapped in paper or card so there's less plastic waste at home.

1

Use the same **shopping bags** more than once.

2

Make sure your **water bottle** is one you can **reuse** again and again!

3

Look for the **recyclable** symbol on things you buy. Then help to **sort** the **recycling** from the rubbish at home.

4

Try not to **waste food** or materials. You can put food waste in a **compost bin**.

5

Do your own **up-cycling**! Use **old** items to make **new** ones.

WOW!

Look, you're an ecologist!

Awesome ecologists (like you) use their **brains**, their **creativity**, and all their **senses** to explore the **amazing world** around them and make it a little **happier**.

Why do things happen?

Ecologists use their senses to understand what is happening in nature. It's all about watching and learning from the world around us.

How do we protect nature?

Ecologists work hard to protect nature. From designing a home for minibeasts to crafting a feeder for birds, there are endless ways for you to protect nature too.

Is that new?

Ecologists spend their time out and about in nature, so they discover new plants, fungi, and animals all the time! Be sure to keep your eyes open – you never know what you might find.

Don't give up!

It's okay if something you create to help nature doesn't work on the first try. Keep watching the world around you and trying new approaches until you find one that works.

Try to think of other ways to help the plants and animals in the area around your home.

Well done! You're an ecologist!

Index